GETTING TO KNOW THE WORLD'S GREATEST ARTISTS

DIEGO
VELÁZQUEZ

WRITTEN AND ILLUSTRATED BY MIKE VENEZIA

CHILDREN'S PRESS®
A DIVISION OF SCHOLASTIC INC.
NEW YORK   TORONTO   LONDON   AUCKLAND   SYDNEY
MEXICO CITY   NEW DELHI   HONG KONG
DANBURY, CONNECTICUT

For Jeannine. Thank you for your never-ending support, encouragement, and advice. Love always, Mike.

Cover: *Prince Balthasar Carlos on Horseback,* by Diego Rodriguez de Silva y Velázquez. c.1635, oil on canvas, 209 x 173 cm. © Bridgeman Art Library International Ltd., London/New York/ Museo del Prado, Madrid, Spain.

Colorist for illustrations: Dave Ludwig

Library of Congress Cataloging-in-Publication Data

Venezia, Mike.
  Diego Velázquez / written and illustrated by Mike Venezia.
     p. cm. — (Getting to know the world's greatest artists)
  Summary: Describes the life and career of the seventeenth-century
Spanish artist famous for his portraits of royalty.
  ISBN 0-516-22580-4 (lib. bdg.)   0-516-26980-1 (pbk.)
  1. Velázquez, Diego, 1599-1660—Juvenile literature. 2.
Painters—Spain—Biography—Juvenile literature. [1. Velázquez, Diego,
1599-1660. 2. Artists. 3. Painting, Spanish. 4. Painting, Modern. 5. Art
appreciation.] I. Title.
  ND813.V4V46 2004
  759.6—dc21
                                        2003004590

CHILDREN'S PRESS and associated logos are trademarks
and or registered trademarks of Scholastic Library Publishing.
SCHOLASTIC and associated logos are trademarks and or
registered trademarks of Scholastic Inc.

1 2 3 4 5 6 7 8 9 10 R 13 12 11 10 09 08 07 06 05 04

Diego Rodriguez de Silva y Velázquez was born in Seville, Spain, in 1599. Velázquez spent most of his life painting portraits of the king of Spain and the royal family. Diego became a close friend of King Philip IV and was made a member of the royal court.

Prince Philip Prosper, by Diego Rodriguez de Silva y Velázquez. 1659, © Kunsthistorisches Museum, Vienna.

Don Gaspar de Guzman, Duke of Olivares, by Diego Rodriguez de Silva y Velázquez. 1634, oil on canvas, 313 x 239 cm. © Art Resource, NY/Museo del Prado, Madrid, Spain/Erich Lessing.

Diego Rodriguez de Silva y Velázquez showed every detail of glittery royal life in an incredibly accurate way. The expensive silk cloth, jewelry, and armor worn by the people in his paintings look almost real!

It's for another reason, though, that he's considered one of the greatest painters in the history of art. Diego had an amazing way of capturing the feelings of the people in his paintings.

In Velázquez's paintings, you not only see exactly how a person looked, you also can almost figure out their thoughts.

Velázquez could do this with any person he painted, whether it was the powerful Pope Innocent X, or Diego's helper and assistant, Juan de Pareja.

Juan de Pareja, by Diego Rodriguez de Silva y Velázquez. 1650, oil on canvas, 81.3 x 70 cm. © Bridgeman Art Library International Ltd., London/New York/Metropolitan Museum of Art, New York, NY.

Hardly anything is known about Diego Velázquez's childhood. He must have shown a great interest in art, though, because his parents sent him to the best painters in Seville so they could teach him how to be an artist. At the age of eleven, Diego Velázquez became an apprentice to Francisco Herrera.

Immaculate Conception,
by Francisco Pacheco.
© Art Resource, NY/Pallazzo
Arzobispal, Seville, Spain/Scala.

A short time later, he switched to the studio of Francisco Pacheco. Both of these artists were known for their paintings of religious scenes. During the 1600s, an artist could make a very good living creating paintings for the many churches in Spain.

Velázquez spent about five years in Francisco Pacheco's studio. He worked very hard, doing chores while also learning to draw and paint. Diego learned his lessons quickly, and Francisco knew his young student was an exceptional artist. While Diego was still a teenager, his teacher promoted him to the job of master artist. Francisco even began asking his former student for advice!

An Old Woman Cooking Eggs, by Diego Rodriguez de Silva y Velázquez. 1618, oil on canvas, 100.5 x 119 cm.
© Bridgeman Art Library International Ltd., London/New York/National Gallery of Scotland, Edinburgh.

Although Velázquez learned a lot about painting religious scenes from Francisco Pacheco, he really was more interested in showing pictures of everyday life.

Velázquez showed a remarkable skill for painting people and objects in a natural and realistic way. In *Water Seller of Seville,* Velázquez made the crystal glass of water look cool and refreshing. The sparkly drops of water on the outside of the glass and the water running down the side of the jug look almost photographic. Velázquez made the contrast between the dented water jug and the smoother jug as interesting as the contrast between the old water seller and the boy.

If Velázquez had stayed in Seville with Francisco Pacheco, he might have ended up becoming a very successful painter of religious scenes. He already had painted some beautiful religious scenes, such as the one on the next page. But Diego had different ideas. He still was more interested in painting the people of his time.

Diego especially wanted the chance to paint portraits of King Philip IV and his family. The royal family lived in Madrid, Spain's capital city. Francisco Pacheco agreed that Velázquez should follow his dreams. He decided to help his former student get some attention in Madrid.

Luis de Góngora y Argote, by Diego Rodriguez de Silva y Velázquez. 1622, oil on canvas, 50.2 x 40.6 cm. © Bridgeman Art Library International Ltd., London/New York/Museum of Fine Arts, Boston, Massachusetts.

When Velázquez arrived in Madrid, he found that King Philip was much too busy to have his picture painted by an unknown artist. So instead, Velázquez spent his time painting portraits of people he had met through Francisco Pacheco.

One of these portraits, of the famous Spanish poet Luis de Góngora, got Velázquez a lot of attention. After King Philip heard about it, he decided he wanted Velázquez to do his portrait after all.

Portraits were very important to European kings and queens. A portrait could show off a person's power and wealth. It could also make someone look handsome or beautiful, even if they weren't that way in real life. Sometimes, when kings, queens, or court officials were too busy to attend an event, they would send portraits of themselves instead!

King Philip was only eighteen years old when he agreed to have his portrait done by Diego Velázquez. Velázquez was only twenty-four. Both men were very young to have such important jobs. Velázquez and Philip both loved art and got along very well right from the start.

Philip IV of Spain, by Diego Rodriguez de Silva y Velázquez. c. 1626, oil on canvas, 201 x 102 cm.
© Bridgeman Art Library International Ltd., London/New York/Museo del Prado, Madrid, Spain.

Philip was so pleased with Velázquez that
he decided to make him his official court
painter. From then on, he wanted only
Velázquez to do his portraits. Diego ended
up spending thirty-seven years as an artist
in the royal court of Philip IV.

As a court painter, Velázquez knew he had to follow certain rules. This didn't bother him very much, though. Diego always found a way to experiment with his ideas and painting style while making the royal family look great.

Velázquez loved working on every part of a scene. He enjoyed painting royal outfits as much as royal faces. Some of the clothing of the time might seem odd today—especially the incredibly wide skirts that were popular at the time.

The Forge of Vulcan, by Diego Rodriguez de Silva y Velázquez. 1630, oil on canvas, 223 x 290 cm.
© Art Resource, NY/Museo del Prado, Madrid, Spain/Erich Lessing.

The king sometimes asked Velázquez to paint mythological or religious scenes. Velázquez was probably glad to take a break from his royal portrait job. He also took time out to do portraits of some of the many court entertainers the king kept at his palace.

Don Sebastian de Morra, by Diego Rodriguez de Silva y Velázquez. 1645, oil on canvas, 106 x 81 cm. © Bridgeman Art Library International Ltd., London/New York/Museo del Prado, Madrid, Spain.

The Jester Juan Calabazas, by Diego Rodriguez de Silva y Velázquez. 1639, oil on canvas, 106 x 83 cm. © Bridgeman Art Library International Ltd., London/New York/Museo del Prado, Madrid, Spain.

These entertainers were called fools, buffoons, or jesters. Velázquez's portraits of these people are some of his most amazing paintings. Some kings and queens in Europe mistreated and made fun of the entertainers they kept around. Velázquez never made fun of these people. He showed them as real people with feelings that were just as important as anyone else's.

23

Equestrian Portrait of King Philip IV, by Diego Rodriguez de Silva y Velázquez. 1635, oil on canvas, 300 x 314 cm. © Art Resource, NY/Museo del Prado, Madrid, Spain/Erich Lessing.

The king kept Velázquez very busy. He even made him head decorator of his many huge palaces. Velázquez had to fill these palaces with both his own paintings and those of other artists he selected.

For one palace, Velázquez did separate portraits of King Philip, Queen Isabella, and the five-year-old prince, Balthasar Carlos.

Isabella of Bourbon on Horseback, by Diego Rodriguez de Silva y Velázquez. 1636, oil on canvas, 301 x 314 cm. © Art Resource, NY/Museo del Prado, Madrid, Spain/Scala.

These masterpieces show Velázquez's special talent for painting both people and horses. The reason Prince Balthasar's pony looks so plump is that the painting was made to hang high above an entrance. If you hold the picture of this painting high over your head and tilt it away from you, you'll see that the pony starts to look normal.

Philip IV, King of Spain, with Hunting Dog, by Diego Rodriguez de Silva y Velázquez. 1634-1636, oil on canvas, 191 x 126 cm. © Art Resource, NY/Museo del Prado, Madrid, Spain/Erich Lessing.

Sometimes King Philip brought Velázquez along on hunting trips or even when he went into battle. That way the king could have his portrait done while he took a break from his activities.

Diego Rodriquez de Silva y Velázquez's most famous painting is *Las Meninas,* which means "The Maids of Honor." Some art experts have called it the greatest of all paintings.

No one is quite sure what the scene is all about. In one of his few self-portraits, Velázquez himself appears behind a large canvas. He's waiting to paint someone. It could be the king and queen. Their reflections are seen in a mirror at the back of the room. Perhaps it is the Princess Margarita, who is standing in the center of the scene.

Whomever Velázquez is about to paint will be standing right where you are when you look at this life-sized painting. This makes you feel a little like you're part of the royal group.

Las Meninas, by Diego Rodriguez de Silva y Velázquez. c. 1656, oil on canvas, 316 x 276 cm.
© Bridgeman Art Library International Ltd., London/New York/Museo del Prado, Madrid, Spain.

Up close, you can see that Velázquez used quick, loose brushstrokes in *Las Meninas*. As you move back, the people in the painting come into focus and seem very lifelike. Everyone in this painting is shown in a beautiful, soft light.

Detail from *Las Meninas* (the brooch of Infanta Margarita), by Diego Rodriguez de Silva y Velázquez. c. 1656, oil on canvas, 316 x 276 cm. © Bridgeman Art Library International Ltd., London/New York/Museo del Prado, Madrid, Spain.

It's possible that Velázquez painted this wonderful picture for himself. He may have wanted to show the world that he was a great artist who was important enough to be a friend of the king and the king's family. In *Las Meninas*, Velázquez captured a moment of life in a way that had never quite been done before and has rarely been done since.

Diego Velázquez died in 1660 at the age of sixty-one. He was both a great artist and a loyal member of King Philip IV's court. Near the end of his life, Diego Velázquez was made a knight in Spain's royal court. Whether he painted portraits, everyday objects, or royal pets, Diego Velázquez made his subjects look incredibly beautiful and natural.

Works of art in this book can be seen at the following places:

Galleria Doria Pamphilj, Rome

Kunsthistorisches Museum, Vienna

Louvre, Paris

Metropolitan Museum of Art, New York

Museo del Prado, Madrid

Museum of Fine Arts, Boston

National Gallery of Scotland, Edinburgh

Palazzo Arzobispal, Seville

Uffizi Gallery, Florence

Victoria and Albert Museum, London